Sea and Sand

Some useful hints for colouring:

- Apply colours only faintly at first - it is easy to add more layers of colour later on, whereas it is often impossible to lighten colours once they have been applied.

- Bear in mind that objects and colours in the distance usually appear fainter than the foreground. Similarly, violet, light blue and lilac can evoke the impression of distance, whereas a reddish tinge often helps to underline the foreground. You may wish to begin the colouring in the sky, then work your way from the distance into the foreground, moving down the page. One advantage is also that your hand is less likely to smudge sections of the picture which you have coloured in already.

- Remember, where - on the picture - the sunlight comes from and in which direction the shadows must fall!

- Try to use several different tones of a given colour; any large area of just one colour can easily appear "dead" or artificial. Experiment by mixing different colours to make the scenery come alive.

- Do not underestimate the importance of leaving highlights white or light, even if they are only small. On wet pebbles for instance, a bright spot will be the reflection of the main light source and will help to let the stone appear three dimensional. Similarly, leave white or bright streaks and dots on moving water to emphasize reflecting sunlight.

- Enjoy colouring the pictures!

Published by : W. F. Graham (Northampton) Ltd. NN3 6RT,
www.wfgraham.co.uk,   Email: books@wfgraham.co.uk
Designed and illustrated by: Henrike Petzl, www.henrikepetzl.co.uk, email: henrike.petzl@tiscali.co.uk

Lee Bay near Lynton, Devon

Giant's Causeway, Northern Ireland

Boat off Felixstowe, Suffolk

© Pembrokeshire Coast

Cornish Coast

Marloes Sands, Pembrokeshire

Spurn Head, Humberside

Near Achiltibuie, Scotland